WORKING FAITH WORKS!
STUDY GUIDE

*The Secret to Effortless Success and Triumphant
Living Through Working Faith*

T. A. KOONCE

authorHOUSE®

AuthorHouse™
1663 Liberty Drive
Bloomington, IN 47403
www.authorhouse.com
Phone: 1 (800) 839-8640

Published by AuthorHouse 04/30/2016

ISBN: 978-1-5246-0590-2 (sc)
ISBN: 978-1-5246-0589-6 (e)

Library of Congress Control Number: 2016906892

Print information available on the last page.

Any people depicted in stock imagery provided by Thinkstock are models,
and such images are being used for illustrative purposes only.
Certain stock imagery © Thinkstock.

This book is printed on acid-free paper.

Because of the dynamic nature of the Internet, any web addresses or links contained in this book may have changed since publication and may no longer be valid. The views expressed in this work are solely those of the author and do not necessarily reflect the views of the publisher, and the publisher hereby disclaims any responsibility for them.

Unless otherwise indicated, all scripture quotations are taken from the New King James Version of the Holy Bible. Copyright 1979, 1980, 1982, 1986, 1994, by the Moody Bible Institute of Chicago. Moody Publishers by permission.

Scripture notations are taken from the King James Version of the Holy Bible unless otherwise noted.

Scripture notations marked (Amp) are taken from the Amplified Bible, copyright 1958, and 1987 by the Lockman Foundation, La Habra, California with permission.

Table of Contents

Introduction

Using This Study Guide

The purpose of this workbook is to reinforce the principles taught in my book, Working Faith Works. You will need a copy of Working Faith Works to work through this study guide.

You will find that this study guide is written in question and answer format. By reading a chapter in Working Faith Works, the designated scripture verses, then answering questions in the corresponding chapter of the study guide, you will gain a deeper comprehension of the principles and learn more easily how to incorporate them as you exercise your faith.

To use this workbook, look up the corresponding chapter in Working Faith Works and read it. Next look up in your bible the scriptures designated in the workbook and read them. This is a critical step because those scriptures are the foundation of the teaching in that particular chapter and are taken directly from that chapter. I have noted the scriptures in Working Faith Works also however, it is better for you to look them up in your bible so that you will know that it is what the bible says.

Answer the questions in the workbook referring to the appropriate chapter in Working Faith Works. After you have answered the questions in the chapter turn to the back of the study guide and use the answer key to check your answers.

Be sure to pace yourself and work at a pace that is comfortable for you. Remain in each chapter until you feel you have mastered it or until you feel that you have a good understanding of the material and how to apply it in your daily walk of faith.

Work your way through the study guide following these steps with each chapter.

This workbook can be used for group discussions, bible studies or individual study. If you are using this workbook in a group setting discuss your answers and learn how to apply these principles also gleaning from the experiences of others.

The Working Faith Works Study Guide will help you renew your mind to God's word and transform your way of thinking and acting as well.

I pray that working through this study guide, along with the book, Working Faith Works will settle and establish you in the faith. Exercising faith in a practical way is easy, yet it requires time because it is a process, however it is no struggle and definitely worth your effort.

Chapter One

The Free Gift of Faith is Dealt To Every Believer

Chapter One

The Free Gift of Faith is Dealt To Every Believer

In the book Working Faith Works, read chapter one first. Secondly, you will need to read in your bible the scriptures listed below and answer the questions that follow. Lastly, after you have answered the questions listed, check your answers in the answer key provided in the back of the study guide.

As you continue to follow this practice throughout this study guide, you can be confident that you will gain insight and understanding that will aid you in integrating these godly principles that will bring you paramount success and triumphant living through working faith.

1. Read Romans 12:3, and Luke 17:5.

   a. What do these verses mean to you?_____

   _____

   _____

   b. Is the measure of faith God dealt to you greater than the measure of faith he has dealt to someone else? _____

   _____

   _____

   c. What was God's instruction to the apostles when they asked Him to increase their faith?_____

   _____

   _____

2. Read Mark 11:22-34.

3. Meditate on Mark 11:22-24.

    a. What is the first instruction given in Mark 11: 23?

_____

_____

_____

_____

    b. What is the second instruction given in Mark 11: 23?

_____

_____

_____

    c. What is the third instruction given in Mark 11: 23?

_____

_____

_____

    d. What is the fourth instruction given in Mark 11:24?

_____

_____

_____

    e. What did Jesus say would be the result of you following his instructions in Mark 11:23-24?

_____

_____

_____

4. In order for faith to be developed, what must we learn to do?

5. What is the state of faith without works? See James 2:20.

_____

_____

_____

6. What kind of faith has God dealt to the believer?

_____

_____

_____

7. Is the faith that God has dealt to you for everyone? See 2 Thessalonians 3:2.

_____

_____

_____

8. When did you receive faith from God?

_____

_____

_____

9. Read Romans 10:17. How does faith come?

_____

_____

_____

Chapter Two

What is Faith?

Chapter Two

What is Faith?

As with the previous chapter, before reviewing and answering the questions below, first read chapter 2 in your Working Faith Works book (What is Faith?), then read the scriptures designated below. After you have completed answering the questions in your study guide, check the answers in the back of the guide.

To gain the greatest benefit from this study guide, continue using this method throughout the book.

1. Does simply believing in God mean that you have working faith? Why or why not?

   _____

   _____

   _____

2. How does the bible define faith? Read Hebrews 11:1.

   _____

   _____

   _____

3. What does faith require? Read James 1:22 & James 2:20.

   _____

   _____

   _____

4. If faith requires action or work, does simply believing change your situation?

   _____

   _____

   _____

5. How do we cause our faith to rise to a level of perfection?

    _____

    _____

    _____

Chapter Three

Working Faith Works!

Chapter Three

Working Faith Works!

1. Read Romans 10:13.

   a. What does Romans 10:13 mean to you?

   _____

   _____

   _____

   _____

2. Read St. John 14:26.

   a. Who did God send to teach you how to apply the scriptures while bringing all things to your

   remembrance?

   _____

   _____

   _____

   _____

3. Read Mark 16:18.

   a. What is the result that Jesus said would occur when the believer in faith laid hands on the sick,

   praying a prayer of faith?

   _____

   _____

   _____

   _____

4. Read Isaih 53:5

    a. What does it mean to you when Isaih said, and with his stripes we are healed?

    _____

    _____

    _____

    _____

5. Do you apply the same scriptures when you are believing God for a miracle vs when you are believing God for a recovery which is a gradual deliverance? If not, Why not?

    _____

    _____

    _____

    _____

Chapter Four

Hindrances to your Faith

Chapter Four

Hindrances to your Faith

1. Can unbelief hinder your faith?_____

    a. If so, how?_____

    _____

    _____

    _____

    _____

    _____

2. What state of unbelief is not a hindrance?_____

    _____

    _____

3. Lack of discipline regarding prayer and_____can hinder your faith?

4. What two things does your prayer life allow God to do?

    a. _____

    _____

    _____

    _____

    b. _____

    _____

    _____

    _____

5. Where does it promise in the word of God that we receive guaranteed answers to our prayers, when we pray according to His will?_____

_____

_____

Quote the verse_____

_____

_____

_____

_____

_____

_____

_____

6. What is a key to answered prayer?_____

_____

_____

_____

7. Name the type of prayer that it is when you are praying and confessing the will of God

_____

_____

8. Are you consistently a)_____ what your Father said about your condition after you prayed, or are you b) _____ your faith and therefore your c)_____with your d)_____confession.

9. James 1:19, informs us that the words that we confess can bring the promises and blessings of God or the _____of God.

10. What is one of most effective weapons God has given us for our daily lives which acts as a discipline?

_____

11. Name eight possible results of fasting and prayer discussed in Chapter 4.

1. _____

_____

2. _____

   _____

3. _____

   _____

4. _____

   _____

5. _____

   _____

6. _____

   _____

7. _____

   _____

8. _____

   _____

12. What was the cause or purpose of the Apostle's Fast?_____

   _____

   _____

   _____

   _____

   _____

13. What was the cause or purpose of the Ezra fast?_____

   _____

   _____

   _____

   _____

   _____

14. What was the cause or purpose of the Samuel fast?_____

   _____

_____

_____

_____

_____

15. What was the cause or purpose of the Elijah fast?_____

_____

_____

_____

_____

_____

16. What was the cause or purpose of the Widow of Zarephath's fast?

_____

_____

_____

_____

_____

17. What was the cause or purpose of the Esther fast?_____

_____

_____

_____

_____

18. What was the cause or purpose of the Daniel fast?_____

_____

_____

_____

_____

_____

19. What was the cause or purpose of the John the Baptist fast?_____

_____

_____

_____

_____

_____

20. What was the cause or purpose of Paul's fast?_____

_____

_____

_____

_____

_____

21. Describe the absolute fast?_____

_____

_____

_____

_____

22. Describe the juice fast?_____

_____

_____

_____

_____

23. There is power in two or more people _____to pray and_____ as it states in Matthew 18:19.

24. When it comes to fasting _____is a key.

25. It is effective to _____ whatever you are fasting and praying for as it states in Habakkuk 2:2-3.

26. How is fear a hindrance to your faith?_____

_____

_____

_____

27. What is a key to defeating fear?_____

_____

_____

_____

_____

28. What is the second key to defeating the accuser, when it comes to fear and condemnation?

_____

_____

_____

_____

_____

29. The _____ is our protection against any and all forms of condemnation and our

righteousness is in Him.

30. When we go to the Lord and confess our _____,

the bible says, he is _____ and _____ to _____

our sin and cleanse us from all unrighteousness.

31. Unforgiveness will_____ your faith and _____you from God.

32. What does Mark 11:26 say about forgiving others?_____

_____

_____

_____

_____

33. _____ worketh by love.

34. Whatsoever is not of faith is _____.

35. We must embrace a _____spirit.

36. God forgave and because He lives in you, that gives you the _____

    to _____also.

37. Let us choose to walk in the love of God, free of the aforementioned hindrances for we know

    that _____is he that is in _____than him that is in the world.

Chapter Five

How is Faith Developed?

Chapter Five

How is Faith Developed?

1. How does faith come?_____

   _____

   _____

   _____

   _____

   _____

2. Faith must be _____.

3. It is important to have the corresponding _____

   _____

   _____

   for whatever you are believing God for.

4. Once you _____and _____the convenant promises of God, for

   His children, and work your faith the process begins.

5. Faith is manifested through a _____by_____ process.

6. We begin by believing God for something _____

   and as our faith is developed we believe Him for_____things.

Chapter Six

Faith is Your Foundation For Intimacy

Chapter Six

Faith is Your Foundation For Intimacy

1. How do you strive for intimacy with God?_____

   _____

   _____

   _____

   _____

   _____

   _____

2. Faith serves as your _____for such intimacy as it states in Hebrew

   11:6. Please read Hebrew 11:6.

3. Without _____it is impossible to please God.

4. What type of communication builds intimacy with God?_____

   _____

   _____

   _____

   _____

   _____

   _____

5. God's blessing, honor, power, and glory should radiate from our countenance and reflect

   or _____His person to _____person

   that we encounter.

6. You must have faith that God loves you to build intimacy, for the scripture says, "faith worketh by___

7. When we receive _____as our savior we receive the full expression of

   God's _____ towards us.

8. The death of Jesus Christ on the cross is the ultimate demonstration of the_____

   _____

   _____

Read St. John 3:16, Romans 5:8, 1 Corinthians 13:7

Chapter Seven

Building Faith

Chapter Seven

Building Faith

1. The _____ is our foundation and without it we have no foundation for our faith. Read 11Timothy 2:15.

2. We must speak or confess the word of God. St. John 1:1 says, "In the beginning was the Word, and the Word was with God, and the Word was God." This verse helps us to recognize God's presence because it is an active _____ in our prayers when we _____ His word which builds faith as we hear His word.

3. When God speaks it is a revelation of His _____and His _____.

4. When God fulfills His word it is a matter of _____ _____for him.

5. A guaranteed principle to answered prayer is to believe in the_____ _____ _____of the one to whom you are praying.

6. When you cannot rely on the word of man you can rely on the _____

   Read 1 Thessalonians 2:13

7. God cannot _____.

   Read Numbers 23:19.

8. You build your faith by _____on what you believe.

9. The word is _____ _____, and _____.

   Read St. John 6:63, Hebrews 4:12, 1Peter 1:23 and Deuteronomy 32:46-47.

10. The _____ was so powerful and life giving that with

    it God created the world, you and I. Read St. John 1:1-3.

11. When we speak the Word in faith it will_____

    _____ what it was sent to do. Read Isaih 55:11.

12. What are the two principles to answered prayer?_____

    1.)_____

    _____

    _____

    _____

    _____

    2.)_____

    _____

    _____

    _____

    _____

    Read St. John 15:7

13. When the Word of God_____

    and _____, your thoughts and actions, it is inside of you and therefore

    abiding in you.

14. When the Word of God controls and directs your thoughts and actions you have_____

    _____ built on the Word of God.

15. Faith can be at a _____or

    _____ degree of manifestation at any given point in time. Read Matthew 8:5-13
    and Matthew 14: 22-32.

16. In Matthew 8:5-13 and Matthew 14:22-32, the terms _____

    _____

and _____ reflect descriptive terms of degrees or levels of faith.

17. If you have been _____ for seven weeks, there is no way possible that your

    level of faith could be at the level of someone that has been building faith consistently for seven years.

18. You should build your faith from _____

    _____to_____

    _____ by striving for desires that are greater desires than the desires that you

    were striving for earlier.

19. If you fail to build up your _____of

    _____ over a period of time it will never work to achieve a greater goal.

20. You want to work your faith on _____

    _____ (things you can handle) and if you keep on working your

    faith you will be able to attain the _____ desires.

21. God has made provision for all of the things that you need or desire that are consistent with

    a _____lifestyle. Read 2 Peter 1:3.

22. When you are building your faith, the confession, "I believe I have received," has to be kept in the ___

    _____

23. Saying, "I believe I am healed, I believe I am saved, I believe my needs are met," are examples of stating

    my confession in the _____

    _____.

Chapter Eight

God Desires to Answer Your Prayer Now!

Chapter Eight

God Desires to Answer Your Prayer Now!

1. God is not bound by _____.

2. Time is_____ to God.

3. What does Hebrews 13:8 state?

4. What does Malachi 3:6 state?

5. Where does God reside?

6. God says, "_____ you pray believe that you_____

   received."

7. Why do you have to believe that when you pray you have received?

8. God does not reside in_____.

9. God has no _____ therefore God is a now God.

10. God sees the end from the beginning because He is the_____

    _____and_____.

11. You should continuously confess I believe that I _____

    received.

12. Your confession of faith must be _____.

13. When you do not doubt, your confession is unwavering and you shall have whatsoever desires you ask

    _____ you pray. Read Mark 11:23-24

Chapter Nine

The Faith of Vision Must Be Cultivated

Chapter Nine

The Faith of Vision Must Be Cultivated

1. First you must have _____.

2. You must develop and _____ the faith of vision.

3. Sight is a function of the eyes while_____is a function of the heart.

4. One of the greatest gifts God bestowed upon mankind was not sight but the gift of_____.

5. _____ sees things as they could be when the faith of vision has been cultivated.

6. When you have physical sight you see things as they are, however when you have _____
    you have the ability to see things as they could be, and that takes _____
    _____.

7. We should never let our eyes determine what our _____
    _____believe. Read Proverbs 23:7 and II Corinthians 5:7.

8. We should allow our _____ to dictate how we envision life.

9. God told Abraham he had a nation inside of him even though he was old and Sarah was barren. It was
    something that could be seen
    _____ in his _____
    was_____. Read Gen 11:29-30, 21:3 17:1-19.

10. When vision is cultivated we are governed by the faith God has put in our _____.

11. Faith can also be defined as, the _____ in the heart or the ability to see the
    future in the_____.

12. Sight without vision is frustrating and dangerous because you have no _____.

13. To cultivate your vision and see with the eyes of faith you may need to change your _____.

45

_____ and or_____.

14. Sometimes your _____ is not appropriate

to _____ or_____ your vision.

15. Sometimes things people say may not_____ or

16. God granted us _____so that we would not have to go through life simply

depending on what we see.

17. To cultivate the faith of vision first we must see with our_____

_____ what the Lord has promised us and

_____ by faith that we see, _____

the word over our situation being _____

that the Lord will bring it to pass.

18. When was every prayer, every petition and every promise that we will ever request answered?

19. How do we pull down every prayer, every petition and every promise from the spiritual realm to the

earthly realm?

20. How can you undermine your vision?

21. How is your vision brought to fruition?

22. Satan wants you to speak _____ rather than _____ things

about your vision so that your effectiveness for God's kingdom will be negated.

23. The vision does not have any _____ until you talk about it.

24. Again the faith of vision is critical because the way you _____

things determines how you _____

and _____, therefore it also determines whether or not your vision will become a reality.

Chapter Ten

Have Faith in God

Chapter Ten

Have Faith in God

1. The chief thing in dealing with a person who is sick is to ascertain their exact position in the faith with_____.

2. _____ must accompany the gift of healing.

3. The second key is to recognize there are times when you pray for the sick and you may be a little rough, but you are not dealing with the person, you are dealing with the _____ that are binding the person.

4. _____ must be dislodged in the name of the Lord.

5. Must sickness is caused by _____.

6. When there is _____ it is necessary to confess and repent.

7. Jesus gave his disciples power to_____ and power to _____.

8. It is our _____ and _____ in the power of the Holy Spirit to loose the prisoners of Satan and to let the oppressed go free.

9. Position yourself from the First Epistle of John and declare

   "_____ is _____ that is in me than He that is in the world"

10. Recognize it is not you that has to deal with the power of the _____

    _____but the_____ that is in you.

11. The final key is _____ when you pray believe that whatsoever you desire you received.

Chapter Eleven

Access with Confidence

Chapter Eleven

Access with Confidence

1. After we are very conscious of developing, nurturing, and hearing faith in Jesus Christ, however we fail to progress towards the greater revelation of what it means to have the _____ of

   _____.

2. Do you think that all of the prayers of Christ were guaranteed because of the word of the Father?

   _____

   _____

   _____

   _____

3. Do you believe that Jesus received every petition and request?_____

   _____

4. Did Jesus ask according to the plan and the will of the Father?_____

   _____

5. Did Jesus have perfect faith in every way?_____

   _____

6. Does Christ now being our savior, mediator an high priest continue to receive all that he request of the

   Father?_____

   _____

7. Is the faith of Christ still in a state of perfection?_____

   _____

8. Will Jesus Christ be perfect in faith today, yesterday and forever?_____Read Galatians 2:20

9. Now does this same Jesus live and abide in you, today and forever?

    _____

10. Our _____does not depend on our faith which can suddenly dwindle away in fear.

11. The faith of Him who lives and abides_____

    us is what causes us to take on spiritual adversaries and gives us the _____ to move into deeper spiritual waters than before.

12. We must_____ and

    _____ tap into and draw upon His bold unswerving and dynamic faith which never shrinks or cowers in the face of the enemy.

13. Where can we find the faith of Him?_____

    _____

    _____

14. The faith of Him is a _____ faith.

15. Jesus had to have the_____ that the Father would accept His life as a sacrifice upon the cross, raise Him from the dead, empower Him to defeat the enemy and loosen the gates of Hell so that he might take captive what Satan had held captive.

16. Jesus confessed his _____ during the days leading up to the crucifixion. Read St John 2:19 and St John 10:17-18.

17. Jesus held onto his faith in_____.

18. Because we now have _____dwelling in us we can know with assurance that we will live in eternity and be raised from death to rule and reign with Jesus forever.

19. It has everything to do with the truth that we have Jesus Christ dwelling in us, and it is by _____

    _____ and_____ that we will be raised.

20. This faith is not _____faith alone but _____faith.

21. We have access to the throne with _____

    in the faith of _____.

Chapter Twelve

Walking in Faith

Chapter Twelve

Walking in Faith

1. Walking in faith requires _____ God.

2. God speaks through His _____,

   _____

   _____, and through His _____.

3. We must _____ ourselves to hear from God.

4. The greatest hindrance that forces us out of position to hear from God is _____.

5. God cannot hear _____. Read St. John 9:31.

6. Sometimes we are too _____ to hear from God.

7. After you have mastered listening and hearing Him, you will find even though your day is busy, you can hear him quietly speaking to your spirit,_____ you and _____ you throughout the day.

8. Walking inn faith also requires _____

   God. Read James 1:22.

9. Just hearing the word will not produce a walk of faith that will grant you the desires of your heart, but the word that you hear will.

10. The indwelt_____

    within us will compel us to obey God's commandments.

11. Walking in faith requires _____ God.

12. Word of God instructs us to _____ the Lord acknowledging Him and He will direct our path. Read Proverbs 3:5.

13. When you can not see your way _____

    in the Lord becomes a true test of your faith.

14. God promises us that we are _____

    in this faith walk if we trust and obey. Read Deuteronomy 28:1-6.

15. The promises of blessings in Deuteronomy 28:1-6, are _____

    _____.

16. The conditions are _____ and _____.

17. Walking in faith requires _____.

18. The Lord is nigh unto them that are of a _____

    _____and saveth such that be of a contrite spirit. Read Psalms 34:18.

19. When we are being _____

    we are being fashioned, molded, designed and shaped in the nature and character of _____.

20. Such brokenness also brings _____

    which also positions you to constantly hear from God as you walk in faith.

21. God will not _____or

    _____ you beyond your breaking point and he will never place a test
    upon you greater than you can bear always making a way of escape. Read 1Corinthians 10:13.

Chapter Thirteen

Hope-A Agent to Faith

Chapter Thirteen

Hope-A Agent to Faith

1. Hope is an _____.

2. Hope is also a _____.

3. Hope is an agent to _____.

4. Since faith is the substance of things hoped for then there must be some hope, or there wouldn't be anything for faith to give _____ to.

5. How do we ascertain hope? _____

   _____

   _____

   _____

   _____. Read Romans 4:17-18.

6. God's word is _____ for you.

7. A goal gives _____.

8. Hope causes you to sow the seed of _____.

9. Words are _____.

10. When you are asleep you can hope because the seeds you planted in your _____ are producing. Read Mark 4:28.

11. God's Spirit knows all about God, and your _____ knows all about you.

12. If you get your spirit in contact with _____ _____, you have tapped the source of all knowledge giving you reason to hope. Read 1 Cor. 2:12.

13. After you sow the seed of the Word of God into your _____

    _____, while you sleep at night, your spirit searches for the wisdom and revelation of

    God in regard to ways and means to bring that seed to production, and produce that which you are

    hoping for.

14. When there is no hope, there is no goal set for the better, although no hope sets _____ goals.

15. When you set a goal by faith that you are hoping for, never _____

    _____. Read James 1:6-8.

16. Hope causes you to _____ the promise.

17. _____ causes you to speak the worse.

18. _____ the word

    will not bring a manifestation simply because you say it, but saying it is involved in working God's

    principle and it will eventually produce the results God promised as we believe.

19. _____ God's

    Word _____ and your faith will grow and you will experience the manifestation

    as you make hope an agent of your faith.

Chapter Fourteen

Stop Worrying

Chapter Fourteen

Stop Worrying

1. Is worrying a sin?

2. Worrying is basically a _____ and an opponent operating against your confidence in God.

3. Worry hinges on _____.

4. The bible says in Romans 14:23, anything not of faith is _____

   _____.

5. God instructs us in Philippians 4:6, to be careful for nothing; but in everything by prayer and supplication with thanksgiving to let our request be made known unto God and the _____ _____ which passeth all understanding shall keep our hearts and minds through Christ Jesus.

6. To keep from worrying you must discipline_____ _____ to think on things that are true, pure, honest, lovely and those things that are of a good report.

7. When you worry that is like telling God, "I cannot_____ you to handle this for me."

8. We need the peace of God in our_____ and in our _____.

9. If God's peace is reigning and dwelling in you, it will allow your heart and mind to exert an influence over your body, and _____

   _____ you in line with _____.

10. Often our bodies are malfunctioning simply because we do not have God's peace in our

    and _____.

11. The way we cast down imaginations and every high thing is by working faith applying an accurate

    _____ of God's Word.

12. When you have thoughts measure them with the_____

    _____. If it measures up you can meditate on it, if not, rid yourself of them.

Chapter Fifteen

Are you in the Faith?

Chapter Fifteen

Are you in the Faith?

1. It is important that you recognize that when your prayer of faith goes unanswered it is necessary that you make sure you are doing the _____ things in terms of your prayer life.

2. If you are doing the right things in terms of your prayer life next check out your

   _____.

3. Determine what your needs, desires and wants are according to the _____.

4. Evaluate your _____to make sure it is equal to what you have petitioned or asked God for, For example, believe God for a bike before you petition him for your own personal jet.

5. Determine what _____ promise to meet your needs, wants, and desires as mentioned in previous chapters, according to the will of God.

6. Ask the Father, in the name of Jesus, and believe _____

   _____ you asked that you have received without doubting as explained earlier.

7. With careful examination, eliminate anything that might power down your prayer request due to an .

   _____,_____

   _____or_____.

8. _____or speak aloud your prayer request daily while _____God.

9. When you speak your prayer request aloud you are mixing the word with _____.

Chapter Sixteen

Five Steps to Execute Your Faith Project

Chapter Sixteen

Five Steps to Execute Your Faith Project

1. The first step in executing your faith project would be to_____

    _____it down.

2. The Lord told Habakkuh to write the_____

    down and make it plain, that he that run may be able to read it, in Habakkuh 2:2-3.

3. Vision is a very precise statement with a specific emphasis and_____

    _____ boundaries.

4. When you see your vision in your mind by _____

    and begin to imagine it, you clearly have vision.

5. _____is a strong image of a preferable future that God has given you.

6. Your vision from God will be_____ focused driving you to change.

7. Writing the vision also _____your focus and

    makes _____on God given potential.

8. Find _____ that correspond with your vision or request.

9. Pray _____ according to God's will as it instructs in the scriptures (1 John 5:14).

10. Have a natural plan of action to initiate your_____

    _____, because it is by works that faith is made perfect, and without works faith is

    dead.

11. _____your faith sharing and confessing it repeatedly as stated in the

    bible (Mark 11:22-23).

Chapter Seventeen

Testing, Tenacity, Triumph

Chapter Seventeen

Testing, Tenacity, Triumph

1. The definition of _____ is to take measures to check the quality, performance, or reliability of something, especially before putting it into widespread use or practice.

2. Testing is used to _____ someone or something.

3. _____ proves your faith.

4. God _____,

   _____, and _____

   faith that has been tested.

5. _____ is an ingredient of faith that demands that irrespective of obstacles you will reach your intended purpose.

6. _____ tested and _____

   applied, says God you are able and can do what no other power can do.

7. _____ says, "I will not give up."

8. _____ is tested, tried or proven which worketh patience which afterwards we are positioned on the receiving end of every request and petition that we have brought before God, left, wanting nothing. Read James 1:3, 4.

9. _____ is an ingredient of tenacity which when combined with faith that passes the test, will bring about your guaranteed triumph every time.

Chapter Eighteen

The Positive Mindset of Faith

Chapter Eighteen

The Positive Mindset of Faith

1. We must _____ between the positive thoughts of faith that bring life, from the negative thoughts of doubt unbelief, fear and death.

2. We must _____ the thoughts that we allow to take residence in our minds and hearts wisely.

3. _____ can influence your actions.

4. Jesus has made arrangements for us to be filled with a positive mindset of faith, placing his own _____ within us.

5. The mindset of faith is the mindset of _____.

6. Be determined to fill your mind with positive thoughts based on the

   _____.

7. The greatest step towards being released into a positive mindset of faith is acknowledging the _____ about yourself and asking for God's help.

8. _____ always breeds negativity.

9. The _____ change of the heart takes place immediately.

10. The _____ change is a process where your mind is renewed by the Word of God as you hear and obey.

11. Sometimes you may need to change your _____

    _____ or the company you keep. Read 2 Thessalonians 3:14.

12. We must always receive the word with readiness of_____

_____. Read Acts 17:11.

13. Recognize the positive mindset of Christ is one of _____

_____.

14. We must be aware how much God _____ us. Read 1 John 4:16.

15. In 1 John 4:18, God instructs the believer not to _____

_____.

16. _____ is at the root of all stress.

17. Satan uses fear to steal our_____.

18. When we recognize how much God _____ us the spirit of fear quickly

dissipates. Read 1 John 4:16-18.

19. Always maintain a heart of _____ as you meditate on God's promises.

Read Philippians 4:6.

Chapter Nineteen

Faith is not a Struggle

Chapter Nineteen

Faith is not a Struggle

1. It is not God's plan for you to struggle, but to_____,

   be _____ and _____ without fear.

2. When we accept the blood sacrifice of the lamb we are to _____

   _____in his promises without a struggle.

3. The struggle comes when we think that freedom from _____

   _____,_____,_____

   and_____ is not a part of God's plan for us.

4. God does not penalize you because of your past _____.

5. All the chastisement that we were due was laid upon _____

   _____.

6. All of our suffering was placed upon Him so that you could work your faith freely without

   _____.

7. Now you can be confident that it is because of His blood shed, that prosperity, healing and deliverance

   from every type of bondage is now your _____.

8. Jesus has suffered and paid the price so that you can work your faith _____.

9. When you learn to _____ that God's word is true you will rest in Him and you

   will find that you are no longer struggling.

10. Sometimes we struggle because we are _____

    that we will not receive the promise in time.

11. Fear is a stronghold and God has not given us the spirit of _____

_____. Read 2 Timothy 1:7

12. Also praising God will allow to take your _____

from your _____ and allow you to refocus on the love of God.

13. The more you focus on your circumstances the more deeply rooted your circumstances will become in

your _____.

14. _____ of the goodness of God.

15. Praise him because he promised to _____ and

_____give you all things. Read Romans 8:32

Chapter Twenty

Persistence-A Partner to Faith

Chapter Twenty

Persistence-A Partner to Faith

1. We must incorporate_____as

   a key component of our faith if we are going to achieve the purposes and plans that God has designed

   for our lives.

2. _____will come against you.

3. Whenever you move you will have _____.

4. It is not a matter of whether God will fulfill his plans and purposes concerning you but it is a matter

   of whether you are going to be true to the_____ for your life in the

   midst of trials so that God can bring His plans, promises and purposes to pass for you.

5. God is _____.

6. _____ means to be true to one's word, unswerving or steady in regard

   to one's allegiance

7. _____ people are generally faithful

8. _____ requires persistence.

9. God's very _____is expressed through his faithfulness

10. God's persistence is also portrayed through his _____

    _____

11. _____means to be unwavering in the face of resistance.

12. When you are steadfast and you are faced with obstacles and adversity it will

    _____ your resolve.

13. _____means to be bold, dauntless and to be willing to move forward

    in the face of fear.

14. _____ also strengthens or persistence and keeps us moving forward.

15. Courage means even though I am afraid, I am moving _____

_____.

16. _____

exemplified persistence when he said, "I will not let you go until you bless me." Read Genesis 32:26.

17. When it comes to working faith _____

people will never take no for an answer.

18. Paul said, "We _____the good fight of faith and we wrestle." Read Ephesians 6:12.

19. _____, which is a trait of persistence would mean to bear up under

pressure.

20. The purpose of _____ is that you might be refined and come forth as gold.

21. Partnering faith with _____ will enable you to deal with the opposition.

Chapter Twenty-One

Justified by Faith

Chapter Twenty-One

Justified by Faith

1. The word _____ means to "make right," when something is wrong.

2. _____ does not mean to pardon, but to acquit and vindicate.

3. In_____ terms justification is a divine verdict of not guilty, labeling you as fully righteous.

4. he law of God formerly brought _____, but now justification by faith through the Word of God brings vindication.

5. Although the sinner once lived under the wrath of God as a believer, he or she now is under the grace of God justified by _____.

6. Justification by faith _____the believer to a place of full acceptance, righteousness, and divine favor in Christ Read Romans 5:19, Corinthians 1:30, Philippians 3:9.

7. Therefore, because of justification by faith believers have not only been _____from all guilt (Romans 8:33) but they also have the full acceptance as sons and daughters of God (Romans 5:17.

8. Because of justification by faith we are now heirs and _____.

9. Due to justification by faith we now dwell in _____

    _____and _____dwells in us.

10. _____differs from sanctification.

11. _____takes place externally altering or changing the persons standing before God and _____

    takes place internally actually changing the very state of the believer.

Prayer for a Personal Relationship with the Lord

If you have received Jesus Christ as your personal savior justification by faith belongs to you! Jesus wants to save you and fill you with the Holy Spirit. Today if you have not received him as your personal savior, and you would like to receive him now, simply repeat this prayer with me.

Jesus, I confess my sins to you. I ask you for forgiveness. I believe you died for my sins and rose from the dead. I believe you are alive right now. I ask you to come, dwell in my heart, and live through me. I will go to church. I will read your word. I will follow you in water baptismal. In Jesus name. Thank you Jesus for saving me!

Welcome to the family of God. Remember you have now been justified by faith and Working Faith Works!

Answers

Chapter One

The Free Gift of Faith is Dealt To Every Believer

1. A) Read Romans 12:3 and Luke 17:5, for discussion. What do these verses mean to you? B.) No. C) The disciples were instructed to have faith in God. Page 2, 3, 4

2. Read Mark 11:22-24 page 3

3. Meditate on Mark 11:22-24 page 3. A) The first instruction given in Mark 11:23 was to speak to the circumstance or mountain in your life. Page 3 B) The second instruction given in Mark 11:23 was to not doubt. Page3 C) The third instruction given in Mark 11:23 was to believe. Page 3 D) The fourth instruction given was when you pray believe that you have received. Page 3 E) Jesus said in Mark 11:23-24 that if we followed his instructions we would have whatsoever we desired. Page 3

4. Work our faith. Page 4

5. Faith is dead without works. Page 4

6. A God kind of faith. Page 4, 5

7. No. Page 4

8. The moment you believed and accepted him. Page 5.

9. Faith cometh by hearing and hearing by the Word of God. Page 5

Chapter Two

What is Faith?

1. A) No. Page 13, 14 B)Because Devils believe however they do not submit to God nor work any works of faith towards God based on what they believe. Page 13, 14

2. Faith is the substance of things hoped for and the evidence of things not seen. Hebrews 11:1. Page 15.

3. Work. Page 14

4. No. Page 15

5. By works was faith made perfect. James 2:22 Page 16.

Chapter Three

Working Faith Works!

1. Read 1 Corinthians 6:19 and A) discuss what it means to you. Page 21.

2. Read Romans 10:13 A) discuss what it means to you. Page 21.

3. The Holy Ghost, (The Comforter) Read St. John 14:26 Page22

4. The sick would recover. Mark 16:18. Page 22

5. He took our infirmities and our suffering for all diseases upon himself and by his stripes (the beating that he was given caused striped markings upon his back) we are healed. Isaih 53:5. Page 25.

6. A) No. Page 26. B) Because you are asking for a different result.

Chapter Four

Hindrances to your Faith

1. A) Yes. B) People fail to believe in you because you are too familiar or common to them. P.30 Matthew 3:54-58.)

2. Forgiven unbelief. P. 32

3. Fasting. P. 34

4. A) Your prayer life releases God to fulfill His promises to you. 4B) Your prayer life releases God to prove to you that you have every reason to trust, if He said it, He will bring it to pass. P. 35

5. 1 John 5:14-15 And this is the confidence that we have in him, if we ask any thing according to his will, he heareth us: 15. And we know that he hear us whatsoever we ask, we know that we have the petitions that we desired of him. P. 36

6. Speak the language of God confessing His word.

7. Prayer of confession. P.37

8. Study the word of God and search out His promises. P. 39

9. Wrath. P. 39

10. Fasting.

11. A release from the bondage of sin, supernatural healing, spiritual blessings, financial blessings, spiritual renewal and it can take you to a utopia in Christ that you have never been to before, revealing visions and dreams of your future. P. 40-41

12. Cause: "to loose the bands of wickedness" (Isaih 58:6) freeing themselves and others from addictions of sin (Matthew 17:21).

13. To undo heavy burdens solving issues that plague our lives and the lives of our loved ones (Ezra 8:23, Isaih 58:6). P. 48.

14. Cause: To let the oppressed go free (physically and spiritually) (Isaih 58:6 & Samuel 7:6). To pray to be used by God to evangelize, causing souls to be saved, delivered and set free from the kingdom of darkness. P.49

15. Cause: Every yoke will be broken (Isaih 58:6) as we seek deliverance for the mental and emotional problems that try to plague our lives (1 Kings 19:4, 8). P. 50

16. Cause: to share with the poor, giving bread to the hungry (1Kings 17:16). P. 50.

17. Cause: That the power of God will protect us from the evil one (Isaih 58:8 & Ester4:16; 5:2). P.51.

18. Cause: Thine heath shall spring forth quickly (Isaih 58:6) to gain a healthier life. This fast is determined for the particular need of healing (Daniel 1:8) P.51.

19. Cause: "That your righteousness shall go before you (Isaih 58:8)." That your testimonies and influence regarding Jesus will be enhanced before others (Luke 1:15). P. 52.

20. Cause: That God's light should break forth like the morning (Isaih 58:8) bringing clearer perspective and insight as we make critical decisions (Acts 9:9).

21. The absolute fast allows no food or water and should be short. P. 54.

22. Drinking only juice type fluids during the fast. P. 54.

23. A) Agreeing. B) Fast Read Matthew 18:19. P 54-55

24. Persistence P.55

25. Journal. Read Hab. 2:2-3. P. 55

26. Confidence is a trait of faith. You cannot have confidence that God will bring your request to pass and at the same time fear. Fear is not of God. P. 56

27. Recognize God loves you and His perfect love casteth out all fear. P. 57.

28. Recognizing that there is no condemnation to them whom are in Christ Jesus as stated in Romans 8:1. P. 58.

29. Blood of Jesus P. 58-59

30. A) sin B) faithful C) just D) forgive P. 60

31. A) Hinder B) Separate P.60

32. Mark 11:26 says, "but if you do not forgive, neither will your Father which is in heaven forgive your trespasses. P. 61

33. Faith P.61

Chapter Five

How is Faith Developed?

1. Faith cometh by hearing and hearing by the Word of God (Romans 10:17). P 66

2. Developed P.66

3. Word of God P. 66

4. A) Learn B) Confess P. 69

5. Step by step P. 69

6. A) Small B) Greater P. 69

Chapter Six

Faith is your Foundation For Intimacy

1. By seeking how to please him or make him your pleasure. P. 74

2. Foundation P. 74

3. Faith P. 74

4. When you have faith in God you will believe and accept what He shares about Himself and also you. P.75

5. A) Demonstrate B) Every P. 77

6. Love P.78

7. A) Jesus B)Love P.80

8. Love of God P.80-81

Chapter Seven

Building Faith

1. Word of God. Read 11Timothy 2:15. P. 84

2. Speak P. 84 Note: St John 1:1 In the beginning was the Word and the Word was with God and the Word was God. This verse helps us to recognize God's presence because it is an active agent in our prayers when we speak His word which builds faith as we hear His word. Read Romans 10:17. Faith cometh by hearing and hearing by the word of God.

3. A) Character B)Purposes P. 85

4. Integrity P. 85

5. Trustworthiness P. 85

6. Word of God. Read 1 Thessalonians 2:13 P.86

7. Lie. Read Numbers 23:19 P. 86

8. Acting. P. 87

9. A) Alive B) Life itself C) Active Read St. John 6:63, Hebrews 4:12, 1 Peter 1:23, Deuteronomy 32:46-47. P. 87

10. Word of God. Read St. John 1:1-3 P. 88

11. The word. Read Isaih 55:11 P. 88-89

12. A) If you abide in me. B) If my word abide in you. Read St. John 15:7. P.89

13. A) Controls B) Directs P. 89

14. Foundational Faith P. 89

15. A) Greater B) Lesser Read Matthew 8:5-13, Matthew 14:22-32 P. 90

16. A) Little B) Great P. 91

17. A) Building B) Faith P. 91

18. Greater P. 92

19. A)Level B) Faith P. 92

20. A) Smaller B) Desires C) Greater P. 92

21. Godly P. 92 Read 11Peter 1:3

22. A)Present B) Tense P. 96

23. A) Present B) Tense P. 97

Chapter Eight

God Desires to Answer Your Prayer Now!

1. Time. P. 100

2. Irrelevant P. 100

3. He is the same, yesterday, today and forever (Hebrews 13:8). P. 100

4. For I am the Lord, I change not (Malachi 3:6). P. 100

5. In the eternal, now. P. 100

6. A) When B) Have P. 100

7. Because God has no other period or time to answer you. P. 100

8. Tomorrow. P. 100

9. Tomorrow P. 100

10. A) Alpha B) Omega P. 101

11. Have P. 101

12. Unwavering P. 101

13. A) Now B) When Read Mark 11:23-24 P. 101-102

Chapter Nine

The Faith of Vision Must be Cultivated

1. Faith P. 104

2. Cultivate P. 104

3. Vision P.104

4. Vision P. 104

5. Vision P. 105

6. A) Vision B) Faith P. 105

7. Hearts. Read Proverbs 23:7 & 11 Corinthians 5:7 P. 105

8. Hearts P. 105

9. A) Faith B) Vision C) Cultivated Read Genesis 11:29-30, 21:3, 17:1-19. P. 105

10. Hearts P. 105

11. A)Vision B) Present P. 105

12. Hope P. 105&106

13. A) Environment B)Friends C) Associates P. 106

14. A) Environment B) Foster C) Cultivate P. 106

15. Cultivate P. 106

16. Vision P. 106

17. A)Heart B)Create C)Speaking D)Confident P. 107

18. Over 2000 yrs. ago when Christ died at Calvary. P. 108

19. We speak the Word of God over our circumstances and His promises over our situations as we claim the answer to each and every petition. P. 108

20. You undermine your vision by thinking negative thoughts and speaking negative words concerning your vision. P. 108

21. Your vision is brought to fruition by speaking words that express what God has shown you because your words have creative power. P. 108

22. A) Negative B) Positive P. 109

23. A) Power B) Talk P. 109

24. A)See B) Think C) Act P. 110

Chapter Ten

Have Faith in God

Chapter Eleven

Access with Confidence

1. A) Faith B) Jesus C)Christ P. 122

2. Yes. P. 122

3. Yes. P. 122

4. Yes. P. 122

5. Yes. P. 122

6. Yes. P. 123

7. Yes. P. 123

8. Yes. P. 123

9. Yes. Read Galatians 2:20 P. 123

10. Confidence P. 123

11. A) within B) confidence P. 123

12. A) Diligently B) Consistently P. 123

13. Within us P. 124

14. Proven P. 125

15. Faith. P. 126

16. Faith Read St. John 2:19, St John 10:17-18 P. 127

17. A)God's B) Word P. 128

18. Christ P. 129

19. A)His B)Faith C)His D)Word P. 129

20. A)Our B) His P. 129

21. A) Confidence B) Him P. 129

Chapter Twelve

Walking in Faith

Chapter Thirteen

Hope- A Agent to Faith

Chapter Fourteen

Stop Worrying

Chapter Fifteen

Are you in the Faith?

Chapter Sixteen

Five Steps to Execute your Faith Project

Chapter Seventeen

Testing, Tenacity, Triumph

Chapter Eighteen

The Positive Mindset of Faith

Chapter Nineteen

Faith is not a Struggle

1. A) Rest B) Confident C) Joyful P. 218

2. Rest P. 218

3. A) Bondage B) Sickness C) Poverty D) Lack P. 218

4. Sin P. 219

5. Jesus P. 220

6. Condemnation P. 220

7. Inheritance P. 220

8. Effortlessly P. 221

9. Trust P. 224

10. Fearful P. 224

11. Fear P. 224-225

12. A) Focus B) Circumstance P. 225

13. Mind P. 225

14. Meditate P. 225

15. Freely and Effortlessly P. 225-226

Chapter Twenty

Persistence-A Partner to Faith

Chapter Twenty-One

Justified by Faith

References

Towns, E (1998) Fasting for Spiritual Breakthrough, Baker Publishing Group. Los Angeles, Ca.

T. A. Koonce (2015) Working Faith Works, Author House Publishing, Bloomington, In.

Ryrie, C. (1994) Moody Study Bible, Moody Publishers, Chicago, Il.

Amplified Bible, Lockman Foundation

Meyers, J. (2010) Power Thoughts, Faith Words Publishing

Prince, J. (2007)Destined to Reign, Harrison House Publishers, Tulsa, Ok.

About the Author

Theresa Koonce is an author, evangelist, teacher and entrepreneur. She has reached multitudes in the United States extensively evangelizing and proclaiming the message of the secrets to triumphant living,

effortless success and working faith. As an evangelist Theresa has impacted multitudes by preaching the unadulterated gospel of Jesus Christ with boldness. She is known for teaching God's word in a fresh practical and revelatory way that unveils Jesus and the need for unparalleled faith in God.

She is also the chief executive officer of Working Faith Works Ministries a 501-C-3 non-profit corporation that seeks to build, encourage and inspire people with the gospel of Jesus Christ, causing them to miraculously triumph over sickness, financial lack, broken relationships and destructive habits today! The organization is also responsible for charitable donations towards the disenfranchised, mentally ill, abused and homeless.

Theresa studied theology and law and holds a degree in Business Administration at Widener University.

Printed in the United States
By Bookmasters